Dear Kathryn.

With love

3/4/2017

Serving with
HEARTS AFIRE

Joseph P. Pecoraro, MD • Rhonda Pecoraro • Vilma Vega, MD

With Hearts Afire Team Members

Published by Hearts Afire

PO Box 14759
Bradenton, Florida 34280

Serving with Hearts Afire

Contents

Foreword

The pages of the book you hold in your hands contain stories within the story of Hearts Afire, stories of people like you and me who accepted an invitation by Hearts Afire...and ultimately yielded to God's call to go! "Did not our hearts burn?" two men asked as they gave testimony of their walk along the road to Emmaus with Jesus. He continues today to cause hearts to burn as we walk with Him. As you begin this book, be inspired to rejoice, reflect, and consider the challenge that you too could have a story that will become part of the story of Hearts Afire.

The founders of Hearts Afire, Dr. Joe and Rhonda Pecoraro and Dr. Vilma Vega, are amazing people committed to serving God by serving others. I am honored to have been asked to write the foreword for this book. I have known the fruit of this ministry since 2007. Having traveled internationally for over thirty years, training and developing Christian leaders, I have the opportunity for personal observation of the integrity and effectiveness of many international ministries. I count it a privilege whenever I can recommend Hearts Afire to leaders in nations where we have valued partners in ministry. I'm able to fully recommend this ministry to those whose needs can only be met supernaturally, through men and women whose hearts are burning to bring the good news of the gospel, serving humbly in the love of God.

In their vocations, they are well-equipped with proper education and experience to be successful in every way. As missionaries to the nations, they impact the people of those nations with the life-giving power of God's love. Serving God in the power of His love changes lives—both the lives being served and the lives of those serving with God's heart. In prayer, Dr. Joe asked a life-changing question: "Lord, what should we expect?"

The Lord said, "Expect to be My hands, feet, and heart. I am there already."

The Lord hears the cry of His people; He sees the needs and is filled with compassion. He fills the hearts of those who are willing to go with His compassion and commissions them to go, to be the feet, hands, and heart of the One who is faithful. Hearts Afire has been faithful to His call, impacting nations, changing the quality of life for many worldwide.

As you read the following stories, you will sense the hearts of people who have responded with their hearts afire, being led by the Spirit of God to meet needs, bringing help to the helpless, bringing hope to the hopeless. You will find yourself drawn into the experiences of each one as they share their stories. As they have embraced the opportunity, God has given them to be life changers, motivated by His love for those in need of His healing touch.

Each chapter tells a story of God using ordinary people in extraordinary ways. You will be inspired as they tell the story of what God did through them and in them as they served the needs of people whose only hope is found in God. The fruit of serving God's call can't adequately express the fullness of joy experienced by those who have seen that Hearts Afire is one of God's answers to prayer. "Faithful is He who calls you, and He also will bring it to pass" (1 Thessalonians 5:25 NIV).

The founders of Hearts Afire have partnered together with others to help accomplish their life mission and purpose, and by allowing their hearts to be moved with compassion, representing His hands, His feet, and His love. Each one is fully equipped and trained to accomplish with excellence their work in their specific field. Over the past ten years, they have organized short-term missions for 673 team members, completing fifty-three mission trips. Expressing God's love in medical missions, digging wells, personal care, food sustenance, the ministry of the gospel, and disaster relief, all of this a result of answering God's call with their hearts afire.

None of this would have been possible without the compassion of the founders of Hearts Afire and their desire for others to join them, to see others' stories become part of the larger story of Hearts Afire. I believe the Holy Spirit is at work in such powerful ways in these days, to give testimony of the reality of God who sent His Son as light shining in darkness. May that light that He causes to burn within the hearts of men and women be ever present as Hearts Afire continues to embrace things that seem impossible, with the help of God, who is known to work supernaturally in ordinary people to accomplish extraordinary, seemingly impossible things. May His light inspire you and illuminate to you all He has for you to learn and know from the pages of this book.

Dr. Don Richter
Harvest Preparation International Ministries Inc.
Sarasota, Florida

Acknowledgments

To our editor, Hanne Moon—You took our ideas that we put on paper and turned them into word art.

To the authors of *Serving with Hearts Afire*—You worked hard on the mission field and shared your hearts with the world.

To Bracken Cox, Hearts Afire Director of Administration and Marketing—Thank you for your enthusiasm and making the book process fun with your upbeat spirit.

To Rhonda Pecoraro, Co-founder of Hearts Afire—Your photographs of mission experiences and team members throughout this book help bring the stories to life.

To Giles Hooper—Your photographs beautifully depict the story of the India mission trip.

To Titus Malijo—Thank you for your photographic contribution.

To Jacqueline Griffin—Thank you for your beautiful picture of Ghanaian children.

To Pat Pecoraro-Stanczewski and Halli Cardin—What a blessing you were by being available when we needed proofreading.

To Christine Dupre—Thank you for using your graphic talent for artistically creating our book cover.

To our global Hearts Afire family—Donors, supporters, volunteers, mission team members. Thank you for demonstrating sincere love and generosity.

And most importantly, we are eternally grateful to God for planting a seed in our hearts to serve.

Introduction

Do you know the reason you picked up this book and why you are reading this page? God does. We don't always know why we do what we do until after it's done. This book was written by people who didn't know what they would experience before they ventured onto the mission field. You will see how their lives have changed, not because they made a decision to "go on a mission trip," but because they acted on that decision.

By the time you put this book down, the way you think about life will be different. You may feel convicted of not acting on your inner call. You may find that this is the encouragement you need to finally jump, knowing that God's hand will catch you. Finally, you may find that others think, feel, and serve others the way that you do!

Serving with Hearts Afire isn't a book that was written this year by a handful of people. It is a book that has grown to fruition from seeds planted in eternity that broke the soil when Hearts Afire became a ministry.

Each year since 2006, Hearts Afire teams have traveled to distant lands to serve people they didn't know. Many of those team members have experienced the pull of the foreign mission field and have developed friendships and spiritual alliances with individuals who have touched their hearts in one way or another.

We have laughed, cried, and sweated together (some of these places get very hot). But always, God's love has won out. He sends us and, when necessary, He mends us. He guides us every step of the way, and sometimes, we don't know what that next step will be.

As you read the stories written by each of these team members, it will be helpful to imagine yourself within each of these experiences. They are not "external" stories that have nothing to do with *your* life. Although you may find them interesting or amusing, their purpose is to inspire you and instill in you the desire to serve someone somewhere beyond your current limit. They are human experiences orchestrated by a supernatural God for the purpose of sharing.

By sharing these stories, we obediently expect that God will stir something in your heart and change you. How you will change we don't know...but God does. The human spirit is much like a balloon that has been stretched beyond its original dimensions and can never return to where it started. So please, sit back, relax, and join us as we share some of our experiences from serving on the mission field with Hearts Afire.

JOSEPH P. PECORARO, M.D.

Be My Hands, Feet, and Heart

By Joseph P. Pecoraro, M.D.

Faith makes all things possible...love makes all things easy.
– Dwight L. Moody

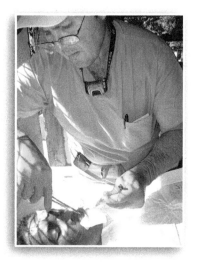

"We need you now! There's no food, water, or medical care. It can't wait 'til next month. We need you now! We need surgeons, orthopedists, anesthesiologists; it's a disaster down here."

How long can you ignore that kind of request from a friend? Why would you?

Fear? Laziness? Denial? Without fully recognizing the urgency, I tried to ignore it for almost a week. January 11, 2010 is a day few people remember. But January 12, 2010 rocked the world and the lives of thousands of people in Haiti. I can still hear the words of Dr. Diane Sabado. She and her husband Francisco were missionary doctors in the Dominican Republic. But it wasn't so much the words as it was hearing her emotion that allowed me to sense the need and urgency. That spoke louder than any voice could speak.

From the comfort of our homes in the United States, people watched with interest and wonder as the "Haiti earthquake" took its toll on thousands who lost their limbs or their lives. It affected countless others who were connected to them by the web of humanity through family, friendship, business, and pure

geography. But when the TVs were turned off and dinner was served, most people in the United States went about their usual evening routines, and in their lives, Haiti no longer existed.

The megaphone screaming in *my* ears continued. I remembered reading that a call from God is rarely like a lightning bolt with a message attached, but more commonly it comes as the recognition of a need and the heartfelt knowledge that you have the ability to help meet that need.

As founders of Hearts Afire, we unanimously decided, in response to the prompting of God, that we must send in a team. Being the surgeon, I was the obvious choice. I never had a desire to go to Haiti. I never felt called to Haiti. But in that moment, I realized that sometimes God "calls" people, and sometimes God "sends" people on different assignments. I was being *sent* on this one. I didn't feel like I had a choice. I felt God telling me, "You *must* go!"

Hearts Afire was an established ministry at that point, and we had taken multiple mission trips to a variety of countries. The Dominican Republic was one of our annual destinations and Haiti was an occasional one. Our Dominican friends were responding to the disaster in their sister country and they needed help. A trip had been planned to Haiti for February of that year, but there was an urgency to respond that couldn't be ignored. From the news, I thought I understood what was happening there, but I was assured that it was much worse.

And it was.

I wanted to jump on a plane immediately, but I knew I shouldn't. If we wanted to be effective, we had to plan. It couldn't be a leisurely plan. It had to happen quickly. When another physician pleads to a surgeon, "We need you now!" it means one thing: lives are at stake and timing *is* an issue.

Who to call first? We talked to those on the ground to find out what was needed and where. We also needed to secure the appropriate disaster response equipment. This situation was a lot different from the disaster drills in residency when we *imagined* a train or airplane crash and did rapid triage without any consequences. This was real. Next, we needed to book flights. The Port au Prince airport was closed. We decided it would be better to get some flights into the Dominican Republic and drive over to Haiti. Francisco had secured a van for supplies and to use for travel across the border. Last, we needed to get the word out—put details on our website, email pastors, and let all the doctors in all the local hospitals know we were on the way.

Thankfully, those who were in a position to provide help from our end responded immediately. I would travel on the same flight with an orthopedic surgeon and two anesthesiologists from Sarasota. Most of the local hospitals offered to donate whatever supplies we asked for and could carry, and our orthopedist, Dr. Dave, emptied his wound care supply room to help our cause.

The flight was filled with an interesting mix of people. Reporters and news media looking to cover the story were seated next to missionaries and Haitians hoping to see their family members alive.

When we arrived at the airport, it was evident that "disaster mode" loosened up some of the routines. It was also an atmosphere thick with tension, fear, despair, hope, and who knows what else! But you could feel it as much as you could feel the moisture from a fog so thick you didn't realize you were in the middle of it until it covered your skin.

Once on the ground, we shifted into implementation mode with safety and efficiency both as important as effectiveness. Much of the pre-planning had been worked out to get us into Haiti, and to Port au Prince, but we still weren't sure where to go from there. Then an email came from a missionary at the earthquake epicenter in Petit Goave. It was a call of desperation:

> There is no food or water or help. Many people are injured. It seems like people are falling apart, and there is more gunfire every night. I don't know what to do. Please pray. Pray for our safety and that food and water will arrive and multiply.

It became clear to us what we needed to do. We needed to get to Petit Goave as soon as we could. I asked, "Lord, what should we expect?"

The Lord answered, "Expect to be my hands, feet, and heart. I am there already."

Entering Haiti that first night was much like what I envisioned a war zone to be like. There was suspicion in the air. Government officials checked everyone who wasn't either one of theirs or who didn't carry some sort of identification that they were on the right side. Our ID was borrowed hats, vests, and a vehicle magnet of a very familiar multinational agency offered by friends on the Dominican side of the border. We were assured that we would be viewed as helpers with that "badge."

Our first night, we arrived in Port au Prince and stayed at a Christian school that had been turned into a U.S. Army outpost in response to the disaster. Without earthquake experience, it seemed that the preschool classroom floor was as good a place as any to spend the night.

It wasn't until the next morning that I realized why so many people were sleeping outside in tents. While I was upstairs using the computer to wish my wife Rhonda a happy birthday, it was suddenly crystal clear why people preferred the outdoors. I was upstairs, inside a concrete building that suddenly began to move and sway like the weak branches of a willow tree in a strong wind. As I hurried down the stairs and outside, I was learning what an aftershock was and how bad it could be. This one was greater than six on the Richter scale.

We were ready to get to work. We plodded along in the van and prayed our way to Petit Goave. The entire way, we saw people along the road with signs asking for help, or mired in expressions of desperation. We knew there were people on their way to help, but we knew that few people wanted to go to the epicenter where we were headed.

During the night, on the hard floor in the classroom, I had a vision of many small lights in the room. I knew they were angels because I had seen this same vision many years ago. The first time I had seen them, they were floating in the room and slow moving. But in this vision, they were not uniform and almost blurred. I asked the Lord why they looked this way, and He said it was because they were "working so fast."

Later, as I was thinking about the vision, I felt it wasn't complete. I wanted more information, so I tried to reproduce it. Then the Lord told me, "It was not you [meaning I didn't form it], it was *for* you." As I tried to go back to sleep, I saw another vision of what appeared to be small black flecks of floating debris in the air almost as if tiny pieces of charcoal or the muck from the bottom of an undisturbed pond had been stirred up and floating in the water. I was fearful at first, thinking these were fallen angels come to disturb me, when the Lord said to look more closely. When I did I could see that it was, in fact, debris. He said, "This is just the dead remnants of the spiritual warfare after the demons have been destroyed."

En route to Petit Goave, there was rubble all over. Some of it had been cleaned up so the streets would be passable. There were concrete walls, portions of buildings down, and one building almost collapsed into the street. Occasionally, empty lots were full of people sleeping on the ground. In some places, the road

had dropped as much as two or three feet with cracks all along the side. As bad as it was, some people still seemed to be in good spirits.

When we arrived in Petit Goave, the look of relief on the missionary's face couldn't be described. There just isn't a word that includes ecstasy, happiness, relief, love, discovery that someone cares, and a host of other emotions all wrapped together in a bucket of tears. There was only a small amount of food at the makeshift market in the area and no stores were open yet. No gas stations were open either, for fear of theft. Now the real work was to begin.

We visited an outdoor clinic run by Midwestern doctors and their assistants, right next to the American missionary's house. They were holding a medical clinic, but there were many conditions beyond their expertise—mainly orthopedic injuries, now a week old, left over from the earthquake. Many of the orthopedic injuries were pediatric, so they were within the expertise of our team. Some would eventually need amputations if their wounds weren't cared for. We realized we were filling a great need when, as soon as we arrived, there was a fifteen-month-old child with a hip fracture requiring a special type of cast. There were also lacerations that looked like they were sewn by a layperson in the kitchen.

We visited the hospital to see if we could use the operating rooms. When we met with the hospital administrator, the hospital was completely deserted. Two of the four buildings were completely collapsed and unusable, and the administrator wasn't sure if the available buildings were safe. In order to use the hospital, we had to meet with the leader of the Sri Lankan National Guard, which was part of the local jurisdiction.

Something happened at that meeting that determined the course of where we would work and how God would use us. Mano was the missionary's right hand man, and he was a local Haitian who had grown up in Petit Goave. He served as our ride and our translator. Mano was a joy and inspired us. His attitude, despite everything that was happening, was an attitude of gratitude.

When we met with the Sri Lankan leader, it wasn't clear if anything would really get done, so we contemplated returning to Port au Prince where we knew our skills would be used. Then I looked in Mano's eyes and saw hope leaving and despair entering. When he said, "If you don't stay, nothing will happen and nobody will get help," I realized that God had given us the opportunity to meet the needs of people who otherwise would not have a need met. It was as if God himself had spoken those words. At that moment, we knew we needed to stay, and immediately things started happening.

One of the Swiss first response people came with us to that meeting where it was determined that the structural engineer would have to assess the safety of the hospital. I walked through the hospital with him, and his feeling was that only one area of the hospital was safe to use. He didn't know it, but that was the one area we needed most—the operating rooms.

The Swiss arranged for Polish Emergency Medical Technicians (EMTs) to put up tents for triage and a temporary recovery room. Then another organization donated some anesthetics and we were ready to start. Marta, a Cuban anesthetist who had come to Haiti in January 2008, ran the operating room like a charm; she was the one who made things happen.

The collaborative effort of countries, teams, and faiths looked like this:

- the Sri Lankan National Guard provided the okay to use the hospital

- the Swiss provided structural engineering opinion and triage help

- the Polish EMTs provided triage help

- other organizations provided medicine to add to what we had brought

- the Cuban physicians helped with triage and recovery

- our team provided the surgeons and anesthesiologists

- the Mormon church allowed us to sleep on their property

Every day, all day long, there were aftershocks. None were as severe as the 6.0 we experienced in Port au Prince, but there was one that was a 5.3 while we were finishing up an operation. Many of the patients were afraid to even enter the operating room, either out of fear of earthquakes, or because of the amputation stories they had heard from Port au Prince.

The prayers for the multiplication of food, help, medicine, and more had been answered. When we arrived, we noticed that God had provided everything we needed. Even the missionary said, "What a difference a day makes."

This reminded me of Nahum 1:7: "The Lord is good, a strong refuge when trouble comes. He is close to those who trust in him" (NLT).

The truth in this situation was, "What a difference God makes." On the van ride in, God told me to "weep for the children" and while I was weeping, I saw a child who had lost his entire family and needed to know that God loved him. Just like the child God had shown me, one of the first children we treated was a seven-year-old who had lost his entire family!

During the day, God showed up again. While driving around town, we saw a touching sight. There was a building that was completely gone except for a woman sitting in her chair with her baby. The crumbled house was around them. As it turned out,

it was the child that had the cast applied the day before. The family was very happy that we took the opportunity to take a photo of them.

When our time of work there was done, we returned to the Dominican Republic and it was almost strange seeing the buildings intact. It felt like such an advanced country after being in Haiti around all the destruction. It's clear that the work we did in Haiti was just the beginning and by God's grace we have continued to send teams to help.

This disaster served as a seed of commitment for Hearts Afire teams to become part of the restoration process in Haiti. Additional teams have been sent nearly every year and have continued to provide medical and spiritual support in a number of different locations throughout the country.

RHONDA PECORARO

Kindred Old Friends

By Rhonda Pecoraro

For we are God's handiwork, created in Christ Jesus to do good works, which God prepared in advance for us to do.
– Ephesians 2:10 (NIV)

The fun celebration wound down and team members spent time praying with the people of the colony. Abandoned and shunned, far removed from the everyday life of a normal daily routine, they welcomed our visit. They lived within the borders of a controlled and confined life, like cattle that are quarantined because of a contagious and deadly disease. Untouchable and unclean—a description that has portrayed them since biblical times. But today, we held their hands both physically and in spirit.

It was Thanksgiving Day. But it wasn't a typical Thanksgiving. Company wasn't on the way to my house. Turkey wasn't in the oven. My mother's cornbread dressing, usually the highlight of the day, was not on the menu this year. My focus that day was far from spending time in the kitchen cooking a multitude of dishes for my family or having a traditional holiday that felt warm and familiar. Instead, we were on the way to a leper colony. The perfect scripture for this new venture was 1 Thessalonians 5:16–18: "Rejoice always, pray continually, give thanks in all circumstances; for this is God's will for you in

Christ Jesus" (NIV). God knew that I would question Him and try to resist this new assignment.

On this particular Thanksgiving morning, the Hearts Afire mission team was on the way to an unknown world. I was scared and only had fearful thoughts as we took our bus ride towards our visit to the leper colony in the Dominican Republic. Could I bear to see the suffering? Would I be able to look at their diseased bodies with deformed limbs and features? Was I brave enough? I had already decided to sit on the bus and just wait while the rest of my team members served there. I found myself asking, "What do I have to offer them anyway?"

As I look back to that day, I remember the details vividly. The drive seemed to take forever. The roads had no signs and we appeared to be off course with no clear directions. With assurance by the local missionary, Dr. Sabado, our team finally arrived at this remote institution, totally secluded from the outside world. The buildings had outdoor hallways with many doors, each leading to a room they called home. Many of them were born right here, spending their toddler years, childhood days, as well as their adulthood in this place. This was their neighborhood community, where they would spend their lives until God called them to their heavenly home.

As we unloaded the medical supplies, the doctors and nurses on our team immediately offered their expertise in wrapping wounds and teaching proper wound care to the staff. The medical personnel at the institution were eager to learn the latest techniques and recommended medicines from the Americans. I watched as they tended to their first patient that needed a wound dressing. I looked at each person with intrigue and curiosity as I made my way to the dining room to prepare for the special party we planned.

Our team put up colorful streamers and blew up balloons in an effort to transform the barren room into a happy place. Guests began to arrive. Some came in wheelchairs, while others strolled in with a contorted gait, helped by a caregiver. Others were in good physical condition with little appearance of the ravages of their disease.

I felt quite awkward and didn't really know what to expect at this party! Could we really have fun? In typical party fashion, we lit the candles on the cake, served each one sandwiches and punch. I couldn't keep myself from staring at them, studying their bodies. Expressionless. Emotionless. Completely unanimated. We fed those who were unable to feed themselves because of missing fingers caused by their damaged nerves. Our special guests peered into their party favor bags to see the colorful things that were made especially for them. It was a somewhat quiet and reserved atmosphere.

The pastor preached a message from the Word of God and my husband, Dr. Joe, translated it into Spanish. It was comforting to me that these people who lived such a hard life were able to hear an uplifting message of hope.

As the music started to play, things at the party began to get lively. Our co-leader, Dr. Vega, asked a patient to dance. Since ballroom dancing was her specialty, she entertained us and included our guests in the celebration. What an unexpected surprise to see them dancing! We all laughed together and we became friends.

At the end of the party, we had a special time where we could pray with the residents individually. I watched as my daughter Ariel boldly prayed over one of the patients. It was encouraging to see her reach out to them in such an intimate way. I walked over to a woman in a wheelchair and put my hand on her shoulder. The disease had turned her hands to nubs. Fingers were missing and there was a blank stare on her face. I said hello and let her know I was going to pray for her. Words of hope, healing, and love flowed from my heart to hers as I prayed a simple prayer. I felt God's presence as I released her to our Heavenly Father's complete care. After I prayed, we glanced at each other like kindred old friends and communicated with a smile. A prayer spoken between two strangers brings hearts together, dispels fear, and releases God's power in our lives in those dark and dreary places. I no longer felt a million miles from home.

That moment allowed me to take the focus off myself. My self-centered thoughts seemed to shift. Less of me, more of God… and I was filled with a sweet compassion for this woman. God calls us to love those who are hurting and are in need. We must be willing to give up more of ourselves so God can become more in us. That's where love can prevail and grow. Acts of service to others require us to take the time to show someone that we care. Do we really care to take the time for someone less fortunate than ourselves?

Mother Teresa expressed true love in these words:

> *Love has no meaning if it isn't shared. Love has to be put into action. You have to love without expectation, do something for love itself, not for what you receive.*

> *Love in action is what gives us grace. We have been created for better things…to love and to be loved. Love to love—to love a person without any conditions, without any expectations. Small things, done in great love, bring joy and peace. To love, it is necessary to give. To give, it is necessary to be free from selfishness.*

We had entered this place, with no welcome sign hanging at the entrance and no welcome mat at the door…yet we were greeted with love and warm hospitality. We were treated like family members coming for a holiday visit. God opened my heart in a fresh new way that day, simply because I was willing to walk off the bus and face the unfamiliar and uncomfortable. What I could only see in the beginning were frail bodies, empty eyes, and enormous physical ailments. God adjusted my eyesight so I could really see the souls deep inside each one.

Undesirable outcasts. This is the world's view. God sees their loveliness and gracefulness. "The Lord doesn't see things the way you see them. People judge by outward appearance, but the Lord looks at the heart" (1 Samuel 16:7 NLT).

To this day, on each and every Thanksgiving, I can see their faces and feel each hug. Compassionate love floods my heart! I view Thanksgiving as a time of joining hearts and sharing our lives with those we love. Even though I enjoy the wonderful food and traditions of the holiday, I feel keeping it simple is always enough.

VILMA VEGA, M.D.

One Touch, One Flame, Many Hearts: Revival In India

By Vilma Vega, M.D.

*Then I will give them a heart to know Me, that I am the Lord;
and they shall be My people, and I will be their God,
for they shall return to Me with their whole heart.
– Jeremiah 24:7 (NKJV)*

*Spread love everywhere you go. Let no one ever come to you
without leaving happier.
– Mother Theresa*

It was an oppressively hot, steamy day as I got into a cramped minivan in Rajamundry, India. I remembered the words that I had whispered to God a few years back when I told Him that I had no plans to ever go to India. Even as I spoke those words, I had thought to myself, *Never say never.* I knew clearly that God's intervention was at hand to change my entire outlook. There was no looking back and no questioning.

India is the type of place you never forget. It is like no other. People walk everywhere in all different directions and by all modes of transportation—from bikes, to motorcycles, to cars of all sizes, wheelbarrows, buses, and occasionally open trucks with what looks like one hundred people packed like sardines in the back, all looking at you as if you were the strangest sight they had ever seen. On every street corner, there is a Hindu temple or a statue of one of the Hindu gods, and there was often a wedding right around the corner with the live clanging of cymbals, melodic festive music, and streamers and powders of every fiery color that you could imagine.

What I found the most amusing was the fact that Indians honked their horns just like we use the brakes in our cars—always and often. As a matter of fact, they go through at least three horn fuses a year. Living in the United States, I did not even know that horns had fuses, but India is a different story. If it wasn't a swerving bike, an overburdened motorcycle carrying an entire family, or an overfilled wheelbarrow, it was the cows that roam the streets and just happen to waddle right in your path at the most unexpected moments. God forbid that you hit one, as you might find yourself having an intimate moment with a jail cell.

After this most exhilarating two-hour, hair-raising adventure, the Hearts Afire team finally arrived in the small rural town of Razole. We would be working with a third-generation pastor family. Pastors Sharath Bhushan and Shraven Kumar each have their own ministries, which work together when teams from the U.S. come to visit. We were one of two medical ministries that year, which partnered with Gospel Fellowship of India. Our team consisted of medical personnel, a pastor, a children's worker, and a camera or two capturing our every move.

In India, everything is about honor. As a foreigner going to serve the people, you are greeted everywhere you go with a lei of very heavy and beautifully adorned flowers that hangs from your neck down to below your knees. As we arrived at the missionary quarters, we were also greeted with big banners and signs that announced our team and honored us. There was no stone left unturned in the etiquette of these people.

These basic traditions of honor and status, when placed in good hands, can be used for good. But by the same token, these principles can be turned around and misunderstood and used to cause pain. This is where the story of one life affected begins.

Latve was a cook by trade, a mother of two, and had the misfortune of having been born into the Dalit caste, otherwise known as "the untouchables." If you know anything about the caste system in India, you know that your status in the present world and in the afterlife depends heavily on the level, or caste, into which you are born. The Dalit caste is the bottom of the barrel. That was one mark against her. However, she was not ostracized for merely that; it was also the fact that her husband had died of HIV/AIDS just a few months prior and that she herself had acquired this horrible disease. Her situation was common knowledge at the orphanage where she worked and in the entire village. That village had never heard of life with AIDS. It was purely a death sentence, and no one knew exactly how it was acquired. The stigma of this disease kept her away from even the precious children that she fed daily. She was segregated from society, with nowhere to go and no way to make a living to feed herself or her two teenage daughters (who she sent away at ages twelve and fifteen to make a living in the big city because she could not fend for them).

That first clinic day, she arrived to see me with her head bowed down in shame. The pastors had asked me to examine her. They also told me that the children of the orphanage, where she worked as a cook, would not eat her food due to fear of contracting this "fatal" illness. When she first met me, she went down on her hands and knees and, while sprawled on the floor, grabbed hold of my feet and kissed them. I felt her shame pierce my very soul, as she would not even look me in the face when she got up. I took her face in my hands and lifted her eyes into mine. I saw that she had lost one eye, most likely to an infection. My heart felt her pain as I reached out to her and told her not to fear. I let her know that we were there to help her—not because we had to, but simply because we loved her.

In that moment, I knew what Jesus must have felt when He spoke about the least of these. After all, we are the hands and feet of Jesus. There is no description for the silent, emotional outcry that comes from one look in the eyes of a broken and hopeless woman who wishes she had never been born. Just the mere fact that I touched her in love and without fear was enough to bring a spark of hope, evidenced by the silent tears that fell from her eyes. I could almost reach back in time and feel the presence of Jesus touching the woman with the issues of blood, as told in the New Testament. I imagined how that woman must have wept after one touch from Him.

I brought Latve back to my exam station and spoke with her. She had not received care of any kind. At the end of the thirty-minute evaluation, she received medications against AIDS, pneumonia, and parasites and multivitamins to help her regain her nutrition. We proceeded to refer her to the nearest HIV care center, which was a two-hour bus ride away.

The last thing I do with patients is pray with them. In this particular case, it became the central focus. We prayed for the release of all burdens, for empowerment of the Holy Spirit, and for a renewal of her faith. The local pastors set up a meeting with both the children of the orphanage and the entire community. During the meeting with the children, I sat next to Latve, hugging her and kissing her forehead gently as I held her hand. I proceeded to teach the children that you could not catch AIDS from touching her or eating her food. Later that evening, the team and I set up an entire educational community outreach where we taught the facts of HIV/AIDS, as well as diabetes and high blood pressure, which were prevalent in Razole. Latve was extremely thankful, and the smile on her face on the last day that I saw her spoke the world to me.

However, I did not know what was happening in the heart of Latve. We go in faith as ambassadors for the love of Christ, but we do not always get to see the final outcome of each individual encounter. Upon my return trip to India eighteen months later, I looked up to see a woman with a commanding presence walk in on my second day of clinics.

It was Latve! No longer did she walk with her head down in shame, kneeling at my feet. Instead, this woman walked in looking happy, healthy, and full of vigor. I would never have known this was the same woman had I not recognized her previously damaged eye. She walked almost with a skip, right up to my desk, a big smile on her face. She reached out to me and gave me a big hug, then sat down at my clinic desk and told me what had happened since I last saw her.

She had established her HIV care at the clinic two hours away, and she proudly showed me her report card. In India, as in Africa, when patients go to their respective HIV clinics, they get a small printed report card where their HIV numbers are updated. She showed me that her virus was completely controlled and that her T-cell count was normal. I could see by the glow of her skin that she was doing well. She had put on weight, and even the shine in her hair was back. She was so beautiful!

However, the beauty wasn't only external because she was beautiful even before she was medically treated. The beauty I now saw was coming from within. That's when she told me that shortly after we had left, she had made the decision to follow her divine purpose. She had left her position as the orphanage cook and became an advocate for women. Since I had last seen her, she had had the opportunity to speak into the lives of many women. She had become a house-to-house evangelist—both for the HIV/AIDS cause, as well as for her love for Christ. She was thought to have touched as many as one thousand lives!

She had also gotten her children back from the big city, as her new work supplied her with the finances to support her family. It was at that moment, when I found out what had transpired in her life, that I realized the true meaning of touching just one life here on this earth. Not only had we treated her physically, but God completely transformed her with just one touch from Him. Hearts Afire was simply the conduit for the love of Christ.

I leave all of you with this one thought: If you had been created here on this earth to touch just one life—your child, your coworker, a friend, or in my case, a patient—would it be enough? We sometimes overlook the simple things in life that God gives us every day. It's not just about the mission field, it's that each of us carries a flame that can ignite the fire in someone else that can engulf a whole community. It starts first with the love of God and, from there, it overflows from God to us. It is then that this love overflows to others. If each one of us found that one person that we could touch and love as Christ loved us, then perhaps we would see revival just as I saw in this one city in India.

Since that visit, I have been back twice more to India. I can sincerely say that in watching lives get transformed, I have seen the atmosphere of this region shift. When we first arrived in Razole, there was only one Christian church. Each visit, I have seen more transformational change. One church became ten, and now there are over thirty Christian churches within the city with a population of around 150,000. That is very amazing in a culture where Christians are only 1 percent of the population.

The last time I went, I fell upon a crusade walking the streets, silently carrying the cross. You would never have seen that during our first trip in 2009. Now, instead of fewer than a hundred believers, there are thousands.

I have visited many countries on missions over the years, and few cultures surpass the fervor, faith, and loyalty of the Indian people. Perhaps it is their meekness, their respect, and their honor system that has bred a strong resilience and bravery. Whatever it is, one thing is clear—revival is ever present in India and continues to grow like wildfire. I am just thankful that I was there to see it early on because of the work of Hearts Afire and the ministry partners in India.

DANIEL AMOAH, M.D.

Gratitude

By Daniel Amoah, M.D.

Finally, brothers and sisters, whatever is true, whatever is noble,
whatever is right, whatever is pure, whatever is lovely,
whatever is admirable—if anything is excellent or
praiseworthy—think about such things.
– Philippians 4:8 (NIV)

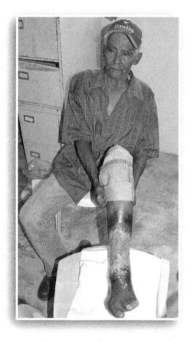

In July 2010 I had the opportunity and the privilege to travel with the Hearts Afire team to Ghana in order to help make a difference in the lives of the people that we served. I was in a unique position among those who went—I had enjoyed the opportunity of being brought up in Ghana. I could speak the language, and I also knew and understood the culture; therefore, I was able to quickly connect with the people there. I could relate to how the people were excited to receive the services we provided.

Some of the things the team did included providing medical services, multiple surgeries, reading eyeglasses, and counseling and offering prayers. The wonderful people of the villages we visited were very grateful for the services we provided. I remember a lady in her mid-thirties that I took care of who presented with complaints of chronic intermittent abdominal cramps. She had believed, based on what she was told, that her abdominal cramps and movements were due to the presence of an octopus in her abdomen. You could feel the sense of relief on her face after we explained to her about peristaltic movement of the intestines and that her abdominal pains weren't because of the presence of an octopus as she had been led to believe. She was comforted by the counseling that she received.

I also remember a gentleman in his mid-forties who came to us with a chronic non-healing ulcer or wound on one of his lower extremities. He believed that his wound was not healing because someone had put a curse on him. We explained to him the course and nature of chronic venous ulcers and the fact that it could take a longer time to heal, even in places like America with very good healthcare services. He was extremely thankful after receiving treatment that included dressing of the wound, counseling, and prayers.

The above people that we served all showed profound gratitude for services that they received. One thing that I always remember was seeing many people with smiles on their faces, living lives full of joy despite having very little in terms of material possessions.

When my wife Rhoda and I had the privilege and opportunity to travel with Hearts Afire to La Vega in the Dominican Republic in June 2016, we saw people in another country experience the giving spirit of the team members. I observed how similar the people here were to those in Ghana; though we saw so many people who did not have enough material possessions, they always had smiles on their faces. The more I think about this, the more it reinforces what we already know—one does not need an abundance of material possessions to live a joyful or happy life.

I believe many people will agree with me that traveling to developing countries or helping those in need can make us realize how many blessings we actually have. In fact, some of us tend to be more thankful for what we have when we encounter people with very little in the way of worldly goods.

On the surface, this may seem like positive thinking. But in looking at this further, we realize that what we are actually doing is comparing our circumstances and what we have with what others have or don't have. The problem with this kind of "appreciation" is that, while it can make us feel good or express appreciation and gratitude for what we have, there is also the tendency for us to compare ourselves with those who may have more than we have (in terms of material possessions), which may cause us to become *less* appreciative, ungrateful, and even envious of others. This can lead to dissatisfaction, ungratefulness, and sometimes depression, all a result of focusing on what we do not have instead of being grateful for what we've been blessed with. Some say that much, if not all, of our unhappiness in life comes from comparing ourselves to other people.

In my line of work, I have had the opportunity to counsel and take care of many people with depression, anxiety, fears, and all types of worries. Most of these people have material possessions in abundance when compared to the rest of the world, but they are chronically unhappy. By the same token, we have all met many people who, although they don't have material possessions in abundance or are living in imperfect conditions, live a joyful life because of their attitude of gratitude. So what then is the difference between these two groups of people? I believe the first group usually tends to think and dwell on the negative things or conditions in their lives, whereas the second group usually does the opposite. This is because we eventually become what we think about all day long. The books of Proverbs says it right (Proverb 23:7 KJV): "For as [a man] thinketh in his heart, so is he."

Joyful people always live a life full of gratitude and in every moment, they always find something, no matter how small it is, to be thankful for. It could be the air they breathe, their family, friends, pets, the weather, their health, or the fact that they can walk, talk, see, eat, or live. Chronically unhappy people will always find something they don't like and dwell on it.

Why do we compare ourselves with other people in terms of circumstances and material possessions in the first place? I believe the answer lies in the fact that most people get their self-worth from what they have or what they do. Our self-worth should not be based on what we have or what we do, but should be based on who we are. In other words, we should separate who we are from what we do or what we have. Who we are is based on God's unconditional love for us. In fact, God created us in His own image. "So God created mankind in his own image, in the image of God he created them; male and female he created them" (Genesis 1:27 NIV). The importance of this point cannot be over emphasized.

Once we come to this conclusion, we will cease all comparisons and their attendant false conclusions, and we shall always express gratitude irrespective of our circumstances or material possessions. Since there cannot be happiness or joy without gratitude, anxiety and depression will decrease or disappear in its presence. I agree with the saying that today's gratitude buys you tomorrow's happiness. One of the most important things we can do is to think through all the good things in our lives and express gratitude to God for that. In doing so, we should not forget about the most important, but priceless, things like the air we breathe, our lives, our family, the ability to choose what we want to think about, our imagination, etc.

Another way of cultivating the attitude of deep gratitude is to be grateful for things and conditions that God is about to bring forth into our lives. In other words, we should begin to thank God for the things we have prayed for or are expecting in our lives. Now when you pray, whatsoever things that you ask for, believe that you have received that, and you shall receive it (Mark 11:24).

Daniel Amoah, MD, a native of Ghana, West Africa, came to the United States after graduating from medical school and has continued to flourish. He completed his residency in Pennsylvania and is a member of the American Board of Family Physicians.

Dr. Amoah is a family physician and certified coach, speaker, and trainer for the John C. Maxwell Team. His passion is in making a difference in people's lives by adding value to them. His desire is to inspire and equip people to become all that they are capable of becoming.

He is passionate about self-development and the effects of thought on health and life. He lives in Bradenton, Florida with his wife Rhoda and their three children Amy, Herbert, and Bennett.

One for the Bucket List... and More

By Mary Bell

And do not forget to do good and to share with others,
for with such sacrifices God is well pleased.
– Hebrews 13:16 (NKJV)

I went on a Hearts Afire mission trip in 2010 because I wanted to share the love of Jesus Christ I held in my heart and soul with people in less fortunate conditions. I desired to be part of the medical and spiritual mission team, which I had observed was doing a good work in the world for the Lord.

I had wanted to go on a mission trip like this for some time, and finally, encouraged by my friends and business colleagues, Dr. Joe and Rhonda Pecoraro, it became a reality for me. I was going to finally be able to check something meaningful off my bucket list.

As my Christian faith grew deeper over the years, I felt the Lord calling me to serve—be it either giving financially to help others attend a mission trip, or going on one myself to serve the Lord in whatever capacity He needed me. This time, with the gentle urging of Dr. Joe and Rhonda, I finally made the commitment to go.

Throughout my lifetime, I had travelled a good deal nationally and internationally. Most of my trips to the Caribbean had been with my husband Dan, to lovely resort hotels on vacation. This time, there would be no resort hotels.

The Hearts Afire mission trip was originally planned for the country of Haiti, but after the devastating earthquake there in January 2010, the trip's destination changed to the Dominican Republic, which occupies the same island of Hispaniola. I will admit that I had some trepidation about this kind of trip—what would it be like to live together in one house with people I had never met before? What would it be like to interact with the Dominican people in a missionary capacity? What would I eat or wear? Would I get sick? What was I in for? Fear began to creep in, but I kept praying and asking the Lord to be with me, encourage me, and give me an extra dose of faith to take the next step.

Flying from Atlanta to Miami, I met up with the mission team at the departure gate and boarded our flight, each of us wearing our Hearts Afire T-shirts. It was fun meeting new Christian friends from different parts of the country. We would be housemates and mission mates for the next week. From the airport in Santo Domingo, we rode by van with our luggage and supplies to the mission house of Dr. Diane and Francisco, their village lying just outside of Santo Domingo. They welcomed us warmly and made us feel right at home.

Our first day of service was with a group of villagers needing medical attention from the doctors and nurses among us, and general mission activities by the rest to help in any way we could be useful. We were met by a happy and excited group of Dominican children, their smiles radiating a warm welcome to us. The medical team and the rest of us sprang into action, unpacking suitcases full of supplies and religious materials for the children and adults we were to serve that day.

With help from Dr. Joe and a few other team members who spoke Spanish, I learned a few Spanish phrases such as:

- Jesus Loves You *(Jesus te ama)*
- God Loves You *(Dios te ama)*
- Obey God and trust in Him always *(Obedecer a Dios y confiar en El siempre)*
- I love you and you are my friend *(Te amo y tu eres mi amigo)*

I sat at the children's low tables and chairs and helped them color Sunday school pages, talked to them quietly, and spoke of God's love for them. Others were entertaining the children by blowing up balloons and tying them into various animal shapes, then presenting them to the delighted children to play with. Others were playing games with the children or reading to them. We followed this by serving them snacks and fruit juice.

I remember the children's sweet smiles and dancing brown eyes, not unlike the reactions of those I had taught at Sunday school back home.

As their sweet little brown fingers colored the pages of Mary, Joseph, and the baby Jesus surrounded by the hay, farm animals, the shepherds, and the wise men, the trusting children would glance up at me and the other members for our smiles of approval and words of encouragement. They seemed to love that we were trying to speak of God's love in their language.

We progressed from day to day that week. One day was spent in an abandoned hospital where several hundred poor Dominicans made their home. Again we assisted with various medical needs, helped with the children, brought in food and supplies, and later that day toured the grounds to get a better feel for how this community lived.

It's hard to explain the emotional impact of the contrast between the relative affluence we experience in America and the conditions in which these people exist, families making their homes in abandoned, broken-down rooms of a former hospital. Several people crowded into a small area, maybe an eight-by-eight room with crumbling cement walls, most of them open to the outside with no screens or glass on the windows.

Chickens and dogs roamed freely through the dirty halls and in and out of the unkempt rooms. Sometimes it was hard to look into those rooms, not knowing what dire condition you would witness. Some people within looked despondent, like they were ailing. Some looked tired and others looked happy, like this was a normal day and everything was fine. We saw a teenage boy with a white plastic bucket filled with water and a fish he had just caught, surrounded by children peering into the bucket and excitedly chattering about the boy's catch.

Outside the hospital and under an open pavilion, the medical team had set up their triage where a line of adults and children were waiting to be treated for their ailments. There was a thin older Dominican man sitting and stirring something in a large, old, black iron cooking pot that was suspended over an open fire by a frayed rope tied to two wooden stakes in the dusty ground. He looked at us as we walked by, glancing up as we observed him. I tried not to stare. I'm not sure what was simmering in the communal cooking pot (perhaps chicken soup or a thin broth), but by the looks on faces of the villagers gathered around the old man's pot, it sure looked like it would result in a meal that would feed several of them that day.

One day we drove in the van to the edge of what appeared to be a vast caldera (a crater formed by a volcanic collapse), the upper edge ringed by a multitude of ramshackle shanties. However, what I thought was a caldera turned out to be one of the city's enormous garbage dumps, and the people living there existed on the pickings of other people's thrown away food and personal items. There, perched on the edge of that dump was a church with a pastor. The church was an unpainted gray structure in desperate need of repair. That was our destination that day, and there we went to help the people again, to bring much needed food, medical help, medicine, prayer, and the love of God.

I will say that as a normal well-fed American, it is hard not to react in quiet shock that there are people who eat out of garbage dumps as a way of life on a day-to-day basis. But I will say that it is a very humbling experience, and one that made and continues to make me fall to my knees in appreciation for all the blessings and abundance we experience (and mostly take for granted) in America.

On a lighter note, one day Kim, one of our team members, led a group of us singing and dancing down the street, showing the villagers a lighter side of ourselves. Several children joined our line of dancing, laughing, and singing adults.

In the evenings, as we would prepare for the next day's work, I was blessed to be able to get to know the other team members. I will always remember them as wonderful faith-filled Christians who had the same desire on their hearts as I did—to come and serve and to share the love of Christ.

In the days that followed, we visited other villages where lines of people patiently waited for medical attention. We were in one village where we set up at a local church. People were in line and seated on the wooden pews. I recall a young, thin father waiting patiently for a procedure and holding a baby. One of the nurses was called away for another immediate need, so Dr. Joe asked me to help with the operation. We prayed with the young man in Spanish, then began a surgery on a large boil on his left arm. I assisted by handing the doctor different items such as suture material, disinfectant, and bandages.

After the boil was removed and his arm sewed up, we prayed again with the patient. He looked at us with gratitude, relieved but very pale, as if he were about to faint. Some of the other villagers in line who noticed his distress began to make an opening in the crowded line, got him some water, then quickly laid down a blanket on the ground for him to quietly rest until he had the strength to recover. The sweet Dominican people were making a way to help a neighbor in need. I was touched by their willingness to comfort him and care for his baby until he was able. Again I was reminded why we were there, and that these villagers and neighbors were also and in their own way lovingly fulfilling the Apostle Paul's encouragement:

> *Carry each other's burdens, and in this way you will fulfill the law of Christ.* (Galatians 6:2 NIV)

Towards the end of the week, with only two days left, I got a call from my sister that our eighty-seven-year-old mother had suffered a heart attack and was scheduled to have emergency open-heart surgery. I was torn as to how to proceed, but I knew that I needed to depart and get back to the U.S. quickly. With a very sketchy cell phone connection and the help and encouragement of a couple of the team members, I was able to change my flight and flew home the next day to Pennsylvania where my mother had a very lengthy, but successful, heart operation. There was the blessing of the hand of the Lord at work again! He allowed me to experience almost an entire week of serving on the mission field in the Dominican Republic with people who had real human needs that needed to be filled. Then He allowed me to fly home to be with my mother to help her through her operation and to provide moral and spiritual support for her and our family.

On the day I was to leave, a pastor friend of Dr. Diane's drove me to the airport and gave me one of his praise song CDs that he had recorded. We didn't communicate too well as my Spanish was as patchy as his English, but somehow we communicated our mutual love for Jesus Christ and the desire to share it with the poorest of the poor people there.

Some of the take-aways from the mission trip for me were:

- There are people everywhere with real needs looking for evidence of the love of God in their lives.

- I know that I am truly blessed far beyond what I thought, even before I went on the mission trip.

- I yearn for others to experience mission work, to help others, to give, to serve, and to be helped and served deep inside.

I'm sure I got more out of this trip than I put in. To be a part of and witness the loving, caring, and unselfish attitudes and actions of the doctors, nurses, and laypeople serving others in a foreign land is truly humbling.

One of my goals for going on the trip was to help serve others and to check one thing off my bucket list. Indeed, the larger benefit for me was that my Christian faith has been deepened, and my soul strengthened and satisfied at a deeper level.

Throughout the trip, I was reminded of Jesus' words in Matthew 25:35-36, 40 (NKJV):

> *"For I was hungry and you gave Me food; I was thirsty and you gave Me drink; I was a stranger and you took Me in; I was naked and you clothed Me; I was sick and you visited Me; I was in prison and you came to Me."*

When the disciples inquired how and when they did these things, the Lord answered:

> *"Assuredly I say to you, inasmuch as you did it to one of the least of these My brethren, you did it to me."*

Thank you, Hearts Afire, for allowing me to have been part of a great mission trip.

Mary Bell is a graduate of Drew University with a degree in botany and has continued to enhance the flora in their yards, as well as enjoy the flora throughout her travels.

She is a mother, grandmother, accomplished businesswoman, and devout Christian. She lives and works in Sanibel Island with her husband Dan Bell.

In her Christian walk, she has served in various ways: Sunday school teacher, editor of her church's annual devotional, leader of her church's food outreach ministry, women's circle, leader of Disciple Bible Study, and has assisted in the women's prison ministry at Atlanta's Rice Street Prison. She also believes in and supports several missionaries and missions throughout the U.S. and internationally.

ALINDA COX, M.D.

A Little Further

By Alinda Cox, M.D.

For whoever wants to save his life will lose it, but whoever loses his life for My sake and for the gospel will save it.
– Mark 8:35 (BSB)

One of the most memorable experiences I have had serving on the mission field was in Swaziland, South Africa. I was there with Hearts Afire assisting Pastor La Salette and a pastor on the Hearts Afire team with their vision of nurturing the starving children in that country. AIDS is ravaging South Africa. One out of every five people in Swaziland are infected with the HIV virus. Mothers and fathers are dying. Children are being left to care for themselves and their younger siblings. If they have family members, they are sheltered, but food is scarce. In many areas, there is no fresh water, and water is retrieved from the streams. Sanitation is non-existent in the outlying areas. Healthcare is a privilege not realized by the poor.

Pastor La Salette has established CarePoints in communities in Swaziland which function as feeding sites for children. They are fed at least one meal a day. The women of the community staff these sites. They cook for the children and teach them about Jesus. These CarePoints are, for the most part, sustained by private donations and charitable organizations.

44

I had been to Swaziland once before. It was absolutely beautiful with mountains and plains, and the wildlife in the national parks was truly amazing! To see the majesty of the African elephant and the elegance of the giraffe made my heart overflow with joy. It was seeing God's creations in all their glory! This year was very special because I had the wonderful opportunity of taking with me Evangelist Dianne Brown and her husband Elder Reese Brown, ministers in my church. Evangelist Brown is also a health professional, and it was Reese's first trip to Africa and Dianne's second mission trip.

For several days we had been in 95 degree Fahrenheit (and higher) weather and had seen nearly five hundred people in our medical clinic. Our clinics started at about 9:00 a.m. and stopped around 3:00 p.m. People in the communities would line up to be seen well before the 9:00 a.m. start time. Afflictions of all kinds were represented: severe arthritis, open wounds, scabies, intestinal parasites, cancer, and also the dreaded HIV.

The clinic started as any other clinic did—with prayer for God's blessing and instructions for our patients on how the clinic would work. Our patients were seen by a medical doctor first, then they were seen by the pastors and lay ministers who prayed for them and led many to salvation in Christ. They were then directed to the pharmacy to receive their medications, whether they had accepted Christ or not.

That morning at 9:00 a.m., the heat had already become an adversary. The windows in the clinic had been welded closed to prevent vandalism; however, this prevented adequate air circulation. The heat was oppressive. We had to attend to one of the missionaries for heat exhaustion, and this required water and hydration salts. She recovered, but she had to be watched very carefully.

Our goal that day was to also do a feeding program for the village. We had beef! This food group was a rare delicacy in these small villages. The women of the community prepared the meat and rice in huge iron pots heated over a wood fire in the yard. The CarePoints are wonderful because they have areas of storage for food staples; they are able to store bags of gruel used to feed children and adults that have been starving. This gruel is filled with vitamins and has some protein elements as well.

We were just breaking for lunch when my translator came to me and said, "There is a woman here who wants someone to see her husband. He is unable to make it down to the clinic and he needs help!" I said of course we would go to see him. I grabbed Elder Brown and off we went. We were excited because it was a wonderful opportunity to be invited into a home and to minister away from the clinic in a home setting. The wife led us a short distance away from the clinic down a sidewalk, then she turned and began to climb a steep hill toward her home. The ascent was over rocks and around bushes and prickly vines, and the midday sun seemed to unleash heat that not only baked us, but also weighed on our backs.

Needless to say, after twenty minutes of walking up what felt like Mount Everest, our enthusiasm faded. We stopped several times to catch our breath and to wipe the sweat pouring down our faces and backs. At one point I thought we wouldn't make it, and there seemed no end in sight.

We were urged on by the pleas of the wife who said in her native tongue, "It is only a little further," and, "Please don't stop! My husband really needs you!"

Mercifully, after what seemed an eternity, our guide turned toward a small shack sitting precariously on the side of the hill. The floor was dirt and the wood was decaying, but it stood. In the front yard, her husband lay on a blanket. He was frail and worn, and almost every bone in his body could be counted. A thin crown of white hair adorned his head. His eyes, however, gleamed with joy when he saw us arrive.

His complaints were mainly of joint pain and symptoms indicating a possible bladder infection. I examined him and recommended medication that his wife would bring back to him from the clinic. He and his wife were so thankful!

Elder Brown then asked him "Do you know Jesus? Have you given Him your life?" The old man bowed his head and sheepishly said he had been meaning to do this but had never been given the opportunity. We all said at once, "You can have Him today!"

With that proclamation, our patient lifted his head and smiled. Elder Brown led him in prayer, and he confessed Jesus as his Lord and Savior in the blistering heat on that craggy rock. A small tear flowed down his cheek and the joy of the Lord filled our space.

My South African brother in Christ was ninety years old! I realize that God had planned to send us to this beautiful brother even before the world was formed. His Spirit gave us the strength to march up that hill. The power of His gospel message saved that old man's soul! I am so thankful to God for allowing me to be a witness to His saving grace and allowing me to participate in His plan. I will always remember that as long as there is life there is hope!! And finally, I will always remember that with the power of God, I can do all things, for He gives me strength to accomplish His purposes in the earth.

When I returned to Swaziland the following year, we returned to this little community. I inquired about my brother on the hill. I was told that he had passed away. My heart was glad, however, because I knew he went to be with the Lord. He was in the presence of God where there is joy forevermore! My heart exploded with joy when his wife expressed a desire to know Jesus and she gave her life to Christ that day! What an amazing God I serve!

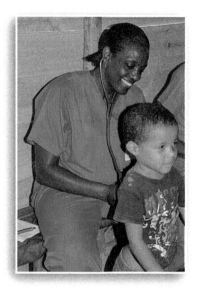

Dr. Alinda Cox began her mission service with Hearts Afire at its inception in 2006. She has been on numerous trips to the Dominican Republic, Haiti, Peru, Swaziland, India, and Ghana. She serves on the board of directors of Hearts Afire and as a team leader on mission trips.

Born and raised in Chicago, Illinois, she attended grammar school and high school there before completing her undergraduate degree at Northwestern University in Evanston, Illinois. Dr. Cox then returned to Chicago where she attended Northwestern University medical school.

Delivering babies has always been a desire of Dr. Cox's, so she pursued the speciality of obstetrics and gynecology. After completing her residency at University of Louisville in Louisville, Kentucky, she entered private practice in Austin, Texas. As a physician with the Austin Regional Clinic (a multi-speciality group), Dr. Cox served as Chief of the Obstetrics-Gynecology service at Seton Hospital in Austin and now as the Chief of the South Obstetrics-Gynecology office. She has been an attending physician with the Austin Regional Clinic for twenty-eight years.

ARIEL PECORARO COX

Stories I Hold In My Heart

By Ariel Pecoraro Cox

"Do you want to stand out? Then step down. Be a servant."
– Matthew 23:11 (MSG)

Growing up, our family motto was "Love Above All." Love and service became the pillars of my life from a young age, and I always knew missions would be an integral part of my future. The stories I hold in my heart are stories of impact, growth, and life change. From the orphans of Guatemala to the smiling faces of children in remote villages of the Amazon, I was exposed to cultures and people groups filled with individuals that I will never see again. However, I learned the enduring impact of missions in the hands of God.

It all started in Guatemala at an age I don't remember. Age didn't matter in my mind then, because I was able to travel to another country and minister to other children that might not know about Jesus or have the resources they needed. We brought over puppets, crayons, medicine, and our full hearts to pour out to the people of Guatemala. I will never forget my first Guatemalan friend, Sindy. Her laugh was contagious and our time together was precious as I shared with her the story of my Lord and Savior Jesus Christ.

My teenage summers spent along the Amazon River in Peru are some of my fondest memories. We would go to sleep on the houseboat and wake up in a new village. These new villages would be so remote that some had never been visited before... by anyone.

Working in these villages was extremely rewarding, because we were able to provide medical clinics for the families as well as Bible school for the children. Washing the children's feet and putting on fresh new shoes was the most rewarding feeling. They smiled at me with their humble eyes, and I knew that the new shoes were just the beginning for them. Their eyes were filled with hope. That look of hope has driven my future mission work.

Remember when you would spin a globe and point to a place you wanted to go to? That's almost how Ghana, West Africa came into my mind. Except I remember very clearly my manila folder with all my research for the country for which I was going to be a missionary. In the mind of a twelve-year-old child, this was the *perfect* place. They spoke English *and* it was Africa. I'm sure I had maps and highlighted pages from books in the library, but do you know what the best part was? I actually was able to eventually be a missionary in Ghana. My dreams unbeknownst to my dad, he organized a trip to Ghana with Hearts Afire many years later, and my feet hit the soil of a country I had researched my heart out for. This country was incredible! The people and culture overwhelmed me as we visited them and saw the countryside. I was especially moved when we toured the castle where slaves were kept before transport to Europe and the United States. It was heartrending to try and imagine the inhumanity prevalent at the time as human beings were put on boats after being sold as slaves. This trip was everything I could have hoped for. And yes, it was amazing that they spoke English!

As a college freshman, I knew I wanted to make a difference. I immediately majored in international studies with a focus in African studies, because that's what I needed to do to open an orphanage one day. International missions is my purpose, and the Lord broke my heart in a way that showed urgency for the other orphans He planned to impact.

My passion was intense and my direction was just beginning. I started my own non-profit with my life savings (My Child Ministries) with the mission to start orphanages. My journey through my first year of college was filled with personal and spiritual growth, as well as full of inspiration. My inspirations began to flourish and I found my profession, and other passion, interior design. This was able to strengthen the vision for my non-profit. We would build the homes for orphans around the world, paired with other organizations and churches.

Six years later, as I dug through my old journals looking for the right one, the leather of its binding felt so familiar in my fingers. *God is Good* was impressed boldly on the cover, and I relived my days in Kenya building My Child Ministries' first orphanage, alongside Hearts Afire. The feelings rushed back to me with every page...

- The white flag of surrender to the middle of my heart as I'm sitting on the bus driving back to the hotel from the site after a three-hour workday on the orphanage.

- Tears running through the dirt face, and the feeling of deep stress making me rely on God.

- Remembering if I ever feel not good enough for this work, I need to close my eyes and feel Africa.

- Unworthy of this calling. If not us, tell me who will be like Jesus to the least of these? Humility is not weakness—it is His power controlled.

As I stood in the middle of the half-finished building, I was overwhelmed with the completion of a dream, the start of a journey, and a hope that I've never felt before. It's several years later, and the electricity, plumbing, and the selection process is in place. The children will soon be running around in their brand new home with house parents to raise them and teach them the way of the Lord.

Ariel Pecoraro Cox is an interior designer, philanthropist, calligrapher, and wife. She has been on eight mission trips to various countries and continents, and is the founder of My Child Ministries. She is a graduate of Baylor University and believes design brings a story to life. Always remembering that each story brings understanding to how well-planned and executed design impacts the lives of people around the world, her skills have been applied both here and abroad.

Ariel lives in Winter Park, Florida with her husband Bracken where you can find her surrounded by lots of friends and continuous laughter. She enjoys traveling, pineapples, and freshly painted nails.

Connect with Ariel:

Instagram: @arielpcox
Facebook: www.facebook.com/arielpcox
My Child Ministries: http://mychildministries.com

MARIA GRACE GOSTKOWSKI

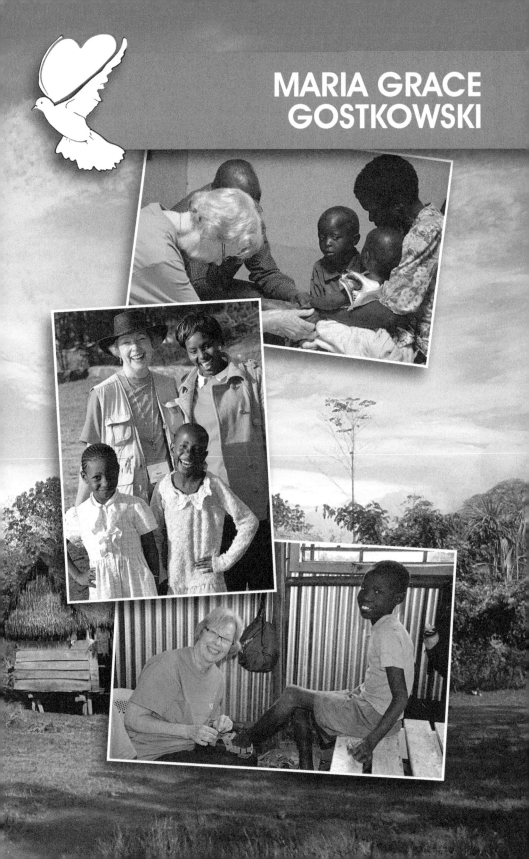

His Plan, His Timing

By Maria Grace Gostkowski

"For I know the plans I have for you," declares the LORD, "plans for welfare and not for evil, to give you a future and a hope."
– Jeremiah 29:11 (NASB)

For there is a time and a way for everything, although man's trouble lies heavy on him.
– Ecclesiastes 8:6 (NLT)

As a child, I ran, frolicked, and stopped to smell the flowers. All the while, I sang glorious notes of praise to God in a language full of combinations of vowels and consonants that rolled easily off my tongue...yet mysterious and unknown to me.

I was no stranger to foreign languages. My first two languages were Spanish and German. But this particular language was different; it was filled with joy. I didn't seem to care, and neither did He. He knew this language, and I felt happy, safe, and secure. I didn't understand *why,* but I felt all of those things and more.

Meanwhile, He was there. He was always there, keeping me safe and dragging me back whenever I came close to the brink of disaster. I began to grow up and put away childish things. Time passed.

Later I sang songs of praise to Him from a hymnal. I found great joy and peace in these songs, as well as a sense of power. He was still there in my life, still keeping me safe, still dragging me away from that dangerous precipice before I could actually fall. But now He wanted me to acknowledge Him, to formally accept His presence in my life. After a series of marital and economic disasters, I knew I could no longer guide my own path. I faced the certainty that I could not handle what life was dishing out. What could I do? Where could I turn?

Once, during an old-fashioned revival, I heard the preacher say, "I can do all things through Christ who strengthens me." That was my answer. I ran down from the choir loft and went to the altar, humbly but joyfully, tears of happiness streaming down my face. I had always known there was a greater presence in my life, but now I understood and formally acknowledged Jesus Christ as my Lord and Savior, without Whom nothing was possible, but with Whom nothing was impossible!

I received the Holy Spirit and found that long-lost and forgotten tongue of the angels once again. At the same time, God put a calling on my heart to go to Africa. I was thirty-three years old at the time. Then life happened. Once again, time passed.

When I was almost seventy-five years old, I was sitting with my friend Linda, who was telling me about an organization that was planning a mission trip to Kenya. The organization was called Hearts Afire, and Linda knew one of the members on the team who was also one of its founders, Dr. Joe Pecoraro. Linda was considering going on the trip. I also wanted to go! Linda called Dr. Joe, and within two hours, we had airline reservations to join the other seven members of the team.

I started experiencing some self-doubt, but pushed it aside. After all, hadn't God told me some forty years ago I was going to go to Africa?

When our team arrived and settled in, jobs for each member were assigned. I was to help by fitting others with reading glasses. As I tried to help those who came for the glasses, I had difficulty getting the best results for the patients. Everyone seemed to want to read the smallest letters on the bottom line of the chart. I had been instructed to use the middle line as the measuring stick, not the bottom line. Finally, a venerable elder lady sat stubbornly in her chair and declared that she wanted glasses to help her read the bottom line because *that* was the size of the print in her Bible!

Well, wasn't that the reason for the mission trip? The medical aspect was to open the door so Jesus could walk in to be introduced. After that moment, the reading glasses were a breeze to fit. You want to read your Bible? Try these on and see which ones help you read the bottom line. But even upon experiencing this success, my doubts still lingered.

The next morning, after a fitful session during my devotions, the doubts resurfaced again. I was sure God was disappointed in me. I felt like I wasn't living up to my full potential for Him. I knew He loved me, but I desperately needed Him to approve of me. I needed to show Him how much I loved him by loving and serving others. I knew I was not doing enough. In tears, I confided my doubts to Eileen, another member of our team. Eileen listened with care and patience, folded me in her arms, and told me not to fret. She assured me I was going to have a breakthrough.

Later, after a busy morning filled with many glasses fittings, Rhonda Pecoraro, Dr. Joe's wife and co-founder of Hearts Afire, came to see how things were going. Rhonda told me the prayer station was swamped and could use some help. I readily agreed to step in and help, thinking I would be sent to relieve another member of the team in order for *them* to serve at the prayer station.

But no, that was not what God had in mind. Instead, I was to go and help *at* the prayer station. I was terrified. *Why me?* I thought to myself. I could pray for myself and others in my private prayer time, but these prayers would be out in the open! How could I possibly pray for anyone whose language I did not know, much less their circumstances?

Then I heard that still small voice. "I would not give you something to do if I was not going to equip you to do it. I have already given you the gift you need for this job." I could speak with the tongues of the angels!

Born an "Army brat" two months and two days before Pearl Harbor, Maria spent the first nine years of her life traveling abroad with her mother, following her father from one foreign country to another. Two of Maria's first languages were Spanish and German. As a career Army officer, her father retired to Bradenton, Florida in late 1950. Bradenton has been her home for the past sixty-six years. Widowed with two children, two grandchildren, and two great grandchildren, Maria retired from county government in 2004 and has spent the past twelve years immersed in her church life and traveling. The 2016 trip to Kenya was her first foreign mission trip, a calling she received from God some forty-plus years earlier.

TONY MURFIN

To Kenya with Love

By Tony Murfin

Once you had no identity as a people; now you are God's people.
Once you received no mercy; now you have received God's mercy.
– 1 Peter 2:10 (NLT)

It was August 2016 and I was back in Africa, standing on holy Kenyan soil where only the faces had changed. For me it was like something out of Bill Murry's *Groundhog Day* as our thirty-passenger bus turned off the main paved road and approached that makeshift Kenyan guard shack that made us all feel a little safer at night. We worked our way back down that unforgettable rough and winding dirt road, the one with soil so rich it had the appearance of dark roasted coffee.

You see, in Kenya you can actually smell the earth, and its unforgettable fragrance awakened me to the clinics, healings, and eternal treasures that had been stored up through the relationships and miracles God breathed out just a year prior during our 2015 Kenya mission trip.

As we approached the property, I could already envision that beautiful courtyard just beyond the tall metal security gate that protected the guesthouse where we stayed just twelve months prior. We were always greeted by friendly Kenyan faces as they rushed to push back the metal barrier with loving hands ready to serve, always ready with big shiny eyes and smiles so bright they could light up New York City.

It was official—after what seemed like two days of airports and airplanes, we had arrived at our home base. The 2016 Hearts Afire missions team was back in Eldoret, Kenya at the guesthouse which I had dreamt of many a night and hungered to return to. It was exactly as we had left it.

Feeling the warm embrace of Anthony, the house caretaker, the moment I walked off the bus spoke to my heart. This year's mission trip was going to be nothing short of amazing. I looked forward to the way God would draw ordinary people together to release the extraordinary fullness of His great love through the divine encounters He had prepared in advance for each of us to walk into.

I unpacked quickly, then rushed over to the kitchen in hopes of being reunited with Joseph, our house chef from the year prior. God had allowed a wonderful friendship to be fostered between us during the fellowship time He had ordained. I would encourage him early each morning with a short devotional to ponder and a quiet time where we sat at the feet of Jesus and allowed His voice to equip and prepare us for each new day. It had been life-transforming for the both of us.

As I walked into the gathering room (kitchen), my spirit hungering to greet my old friend Joseph, I found him nowhere to be seen and clearly not on this year's assignment.

I did see, however, a young man chopping away on a cutting board, so I approached him and introduced myself as a member of the team that would be with him for the next couple of weeks. He replied, "Welcome. I am Kioko, your chef." Kioko, I thought to myself, sounds like the name of a mighty samurai warrior from ancient days past. After a brief interlude, Kioko was right back to work. He was obviously a man of few words and on a mission of his own.

The kitchen quickly filled with hungry team members and my time with Kioko was cut short as he was bombarded with team member dietary needs and special requests. I clearly sensed in my spirit that Kioko was a bit overwhelmed by the challenging assignment ahead, as his kitchen (and a chef's domain) was now filled with *wazungu* (white folks) speaking out orders.

Kioko managed to pacify the team with a small snack for lunch and got started on dinner with a menu that lent itself to more of a local Kenyan cuisine. I could clearly discern at dinner that the team's first choice for protein would not have been mutton! I felt Kioko's pain along with an overwhelming spirit of discouragement and failure, as he clearly thought he had somehow fallen short and disappointed the team.

Dr. Joe confirmed my discernment, so after dinner, the team opened a dialog and began communicating any preferences for forthcoming mealtimes. I could see in the spirit this only added to the lie of inadequacy Kioko was already feeling and believing about himself. In that moment, I knew God had opened a door of opportunity to invest in this precious soul He had named Kioko by extracting these lies planted by the Enemy and replacing it with His Truth.

Early the next morning, before anyone would even consider being awake, I sat in my quiet time, two-way journaling as Kioko walked into the kitchen with his assistant. Millicent had been brought in to help serve us, and she showed up with a razor-sharp focus on getting the job done well—chopping, cutting, slicing, and dicing like a master Iron Chef.

The kitchen remained still and voiceless. The only sounds were two chefs preparing the food with no chit-chat marring the silence. The Spirit nudged me. *Just do it—ask them both how you can pray for them and their day.* Once we got past a small language barrier, I reached out for their hands. Kioko asked for continued work and provision after this assignment was over. Millicent requested prayer for her marriage and family. As I prayed over them, I recall asking God to allow me to see these two beautiful individuals the way He saw them, and He began to reveal all that had been concealed. I began to proclaim His magnificent truths about Kioko and his workmate Millicent— the wonderful way in which He uniquely knitted, formed, and fashioned them, speaking out only the words my Father in Heaven knew they needed to hear to be equipped, encouraged, and drawn deep into the almighty arms of His love and unfailing grace for them.

When God was finished, their bright white smiles lit up that kitchen as tears ran down their cheeks. It was like an unveiling of their identities for the first time, as if no one had ever prayed over them before. No mzungu had, for sure. A relationship was born, and God delighted in all He had made possible. As He looked down upon us, it was very good!

As our week progressed, so did my divine morning exchanges with Millicent, Kioko, and the team members as we began getting to know one another and doing life together. God increased the medical mission as the team experienced Him moving through His children supernaturally. More miracles were being manifested up on prayer mountain and in the small village of Baharini than we could possibly comprehend. Our dinnertime chatter was abundant with individual testimony and the overwhelming excitement that flowed out through the storytelling of each physical healing, each spiritual deliverance, and each salvation experience, all of which were too many to recount. The kitchen filled with the Spirit of Love and Life as we shared our Jesus moments and all God had done, was doing, and would do through a group of strangers coming together. He had called us out to a foreign land, far from home and family,

to glorify and advance His Kingdom by pouring out His great hope, peace, and love onto all those He brought into the circles of our influence each day.

It was Friday night, and the Lord had led me to dig deeper into the spiritual wellness of one of the guesthouse chefs. As I shared all the miracles and supernatural healings taking place up on prayer mountain, Millicent's response was a very curt, "I don't believe it!"

As she stared me down, I asked her what it was that she doubted. Then I knew—I asked her if we could sit down in the morning and talk through what it was that she was struggling to believe.

However, after dinner Millicent came out into the living room. "It can't wait until morning," she said. "Can you share with me right now?" As I shared the great love of Jesus Christ with Millicent, she revealed to me her unbelief was in a Jesus that would allow so much hurt, hatred, pain, and evil to exist in the world He so loved. God whispered to my heart—*she is speaking of her world.*

I took her from the Garden of Eden to the Revelation of Christ over the next several hours. We laughed together, we cried together, and we even rejoiced together. Then I popped the question. "Millicent, are you ready to receive Jesus into your heart?" She shook her head with an unequivocal no!

I was without words! I had just witnessed to the endless miracles in my own life. I had shown her where He had taken me, a child of wrath who believed the lies that kept me a hopeless, self-centered atheist, and transformed me into the marvelous light of a Christ-centered ambassador for the Kingdom of God. I had just shared the entire Christian story.

"What else is there, Lord?" I prayed. God spoke this to me: *Millicent's unbelief stems from the emotional pain of abuse, and she is being held in bondage by unforgiveness. Reveal to her that I have spoken to you in the Spirit, and tell her I know her pain and want to bear it and take it from her. Ask her if she will give it to me.*

I spoke the words God had given me. "Millicent, the Holy Spirit has spoken to me. He wants you to know that He understands your pain and anger towards Him. He wants you to give Him the hurt and deep-seated pain of your past, to know that you are not defined by your past but by the blood of the Cross, that what you have done and what has been done against you have been forgiven through Christ. He wants you to know in the depths of your heart it was never your fault and that He sees you clean and whole. He loves you, Millicent, and He will wait as long as it takes for you to forgive and receive Him."

Millicent began to weep deeply as she fell into my arms and allowed God to comfort her in her time of need, to wrap her in His all-consuming love-blanket of grace. In a moment, He freed her of her emotional pain, hurt, and an unforgiving heart that was holding her captive to her past. These things and more were brought into the light, which led her into the living, breathing, forgiving arms of Jesus Christ as her personal Lord and Savior.

Wow! I was stunned by my Father's indescribable love once again!

The kitchen was spiritually brighter the next morning as Millicent arrived early for devotional and quiet time. I explained the rejoicing and party taking place in Heaven above over her born-again experience. You couldn't have wiped that smile off her face with an SOS pad! It was a glorious day in Kenya and the Kingdom!

I inquired where Chef Kioko was, and she said he was not well and would be there to help with dinner service. However, when we arrived back to the house for dinner, Millicent approached me and asked if we could pray for Kioko. He had been involved in a motorcycle accident during the afternoon and was rushed to the hospital. We prayed together for His divine healing.

After dinner, as I sat up with a team member bragging on God, Chef Kioko walked in, covered in a road rash and with a large goose egg on his forehead. He confessed he had been listening to all God's miracle stories of healing during the week and was so encouraged through our devotional and daily prayer time that he wanted to ask if we would pray for the healing of his body. I had some discernment that he was medicated or possibly intoxicated. Regardless, he was beat up and in need of prayer, so we claimed the healing stripes of Christ to be released over his body. He thanked us and was gone as quickly as he had arrived. We continued to pray against the enemy's attack upon him.

Later that night, Kioko came running up those stairs with arms wide open, as if to receive a warm embrace from an old friend! With tears flowing down his face and a repentant heart crying out for God's forgiveness, he poured out his confession of addiction and proclaimed his need to receive the life of Jesus into his heart. He wanted his marriage to be made right before the eyes of God, and he wanted to be set free from the bondage of alcohol and the curse of separation from God, just like his wife. I held Kioko in my arms as he did business with his Savior. As he shared his surrendered heart before the Throne of God, it was nothing short of glory!

The sweetest part of all is that the Lord revealed that Kioko's wife and the marriage he was praying for God to bless and heal was his eternal covenant with Chef Millicent. The chefs were actually a team of one flesh. Not workmates, but soulmates!

Amazing grace...

The Kingdom was advanced by two beautiful souls, and a once quiet and voiceless kitchen came alive in Christ over the days and nights that followed. The team witnessed not only the fruitful restoration of both a son and daughter, but also the reconciliation of a marriage and family brought back into its rightful covenant with God as our chefs joined the Hearts Afire team for church services our last Sunday in Kenya.

That wonderful kitchen we call the gathering place now echoes sweet words between a husband and wife who have become one. I am thankful for so many miracles I could have written about, but these two beautiful Kenyan children of God ransomed my heart. Praise be to the King of Kings and Lord of Lords for His salvation, restoration, and ministry of reconciliation!

I invite you to come and walk with God as well. He has a mission and plan for you too!

Tony Murfin is the founder and servant-leader of Ground Zero Electrostatics, an international static control company servicing the world. Established in 1997, Tony has been in marketplace ministry from the time he surrendered his life and the business back to its rightful Owner—Jesus Christ—in 2008.

Since his radical life transformation, Tony has had a heart surrendered to Christ for the advancement of the Kingdom and for the betterment of mankind. He has an unwavering passion and boldness to give Jesus away to all who enter his circle, that they may become one and alive with Christ also.

As Tony travels the world on business and pleasure under the influence of Christ, he is the catalyst for others to experience the depths of our Creator's love, intimacy, and oneness. Tony is extensively involved in world missions and has a heart for echoing the life, love, and truth of Jesus as he goes. Tony is a Christian book author, with plans to release his first book entitled, A Father Saving Son, the story of a prodigal of a prodigal, in early 2017.

Tony and his amazing wife Bimini have been married and together for the past twenty-seven years. Bimini is the willing vessel God used to pray Tony into the strong saving arms of Jesus his Lord. Tony and Bimini have been entrusted with three beautiful daughters and a son, making the Tribe of Murfin six in total. Zackery "Zack" (34); Karagan "KarBear" (15); Kiah "Papaya" (14); Katalina "KitKat" (3). The Murfins reside in paradise alongside the white sandy beaches of the west coast of Florida.

CHRISTI VILA

Planted in My Heart

By Christi Vila

Go out into the world today and love the people you meet.
Let your presence light new light in the hearts of people.
— Mother Theresa

As we climbed into the large open-air truck, we each called out a number. There were sixteen team members aboard on our first day out to the mission field.

"Why call out a number?" I asked our team leader.

"So we don't lose anybody and don't leave anyone behind," he replied.

Bumping down the dirt roads of the Dominican countryside, in and out of huge potholes as we went, the excitement and anticipation were bubbling up inside me. Some potholes tossed me a couple of feet up in the air, right out of my seat! Laughter and chit-chat could be heard between the loud roars of the jeep engine as it strained and pulled to get us up the steep mountainside to a rural village community.

We were winding and climbing, higher and higher, when suddenly the engine stalled out just as we slowed down enough to allow other travelers to go by, which I learned was a common occurrence. There is only one vehicle lane in this rough terrain, and the people get around mostly on horseback or on foot with a donkey in tow.

My heart was pounding—we were almost there! What was I going to do when I got there? How was I going to be of help to these people? Would they accept us? So many questions began flooding my mind. *The answers will come. Trust the journey that God has placed you on,* I thought to myself.

From the time I was a little girl, I knew that an almighty God existed. I used to stare long and deep into starry night skies and feel the awe of knowing that He knew and loved me more than I could ever imagine. Although my childhood years were lived overseas in Singapore and I was exposed to many cultures and religions, I accepted Christ into my life when I was in my mid-twenties. However, as I had stopped going to church and was pursuing my own desires, goals, and career, nothing dramatically changed in my life as a Christian. (I call that EGO— Edge God Out!)

After getting married and having two children, God started planting the seed in my heart for missionary service. One day while having lunch with a lady at work, God used her to prompt the idea boldly into my thoughts. From that time on, I couldn't stop thinking about the idea as it became more and more firmly rooted in me. I began noticing the multitude of homeless people on my own city streets. I started listening to news about orphaned children in Romania, about people starving in Biafra, and on and on. I'd ask myself (and God) what I could do to help. Clearly, I wanted to go into the mission field, but first I was led to get my nursing degree and gain experience in the medical field.

For three years, my heart was filled with amazing joy working as a nurse in a rural medical clinic in Florida. We cared for migrant farm workers and their families. This was God's way of giving me my first experience in the mission field. He was imprinting His plan on my heart, a plan for me to go on further in mission work.

My husband was nervous and uncomfortable about the idea at first, but as we discussed it further, he agreed, as long as we could go together on a mission trip. God did the rest. We were soon paired up with the Hearts Afire mission team. My husband, my twenty-five-year-old son, and I joined the team leaving for the Dominican Republic.

Our truck came to a stop in front of a small A-frame wooden building with a church name sign and cross painted on it. We had arrived at the village! Behind the church were acres of fields and within minutes, dozens of people appeared from them, walking toward the church. Small faces peered out of the one little window of the church, children smiling at us as we unloaded our equipment and supplies.

Only a couple of other small wooden huts lined the single street of this village. Where did people live? Across the fields you could see rustic shelters leaning against trees that I presumed the people here called their homes. Several goats herded by donkey riders came racing past us, leaving a flurry of dirt and dust all over my face and my glasses. There was no running water in the village, but a large water-filled container was brought to the church by donkey for us to use as needed. I quickly cleaned off my glasses so that I could see and was ready for what we were going to do next.

Villagers gathered, old and young, into the one-room church. All eyes were on us, the medical mission team that had come from so far away to bring medicine and treat their ailments. You could see the hopefulness in their eyes, as it had been a whole year since they had been visited and brought any sort of medical assistance. Speaking in fluent Spanish, our team leader opened in prayer and then invited the team members to pray over individuals in the gathering. My heart jumped into my throat! Never before had I prayed out loud, and never had I prayed out loud for someone else.

As my eyes scanned the room, I focused on an older woman sitting quietly next to her adolescent daughter. As I approached her, the daughter told me that her mother's eyes were open but that she was completely without sight. I would pray for her in English, I explained to them, and she acknowledged that her mother was a believer and would greatly appreciate the prayer. Gently, I took her hand in mine, and as I placed my other hand on her cheek, a sense of overwhelming peace raced through my body. It was like my body no longer belonged to me but had been taken over by a gentle power that I had no control over. I prayed, loudly and yet tenderly, for this woman's physical and spiritual well-being, as well as for her daughter's. Although she couldn't see me with her eyes, I felt that she received me openly with her heart.

When I finished praying and opened my eyes, she was looking right at me with a big beautiful smile. The deep connection of the Holy Spirit between us both was undeniable—strong and powerful. A sensation of lightness floated off me as I hugged her and left to begin the medical clinic set-up. That moment was a turning point for me. I was reminded that our physical senses— sight, hearing, smell, taste, and touch—only scratch the surface of the depth of connection that God has created for us to make with one another. Through His Holy Spirit that is in us, we can connect to the deepest parts of our lives and the lives of others.

Being a part of the mission team meant long days in the field with extensive drives to get to our village. Most days were hot and uncomfortable. Many of us never experience anything close to this back home. My realization was that this was not so much about bringing the people medicine and supplies, but so much more about showing them the love of Christ and the hope that he gives us all. By the glimmer in their eyes, their smiles, and their hugs as we left, I wholeheartedly believe that they received this benefit. My heart and spirit were filled and lifted, changed forever by serving the people we visited.

In John 13:14-15, Jesus says: "Now that I, your Lord and Teacher, have washed your feet, you also should wash one another's feet. I have set you an example that you should do as I have done for you" (NIV). And in verse 17, he continues, "Now that you know these things, you will be blessed if you do them."

And that blessing is exactly what I experienced from serving on the mission team and serving others, through our Lord, Christ Jesus.

Christi Vila as a child was raised in Singapore, Southeast Asia where she was immersed in a multicultural environment and developed her love of people. She is married to her husband and soulmate of thirty years and now lives in Florida.

Although her earlier careers were in hotel sales/ marketing and consumer banking, for most of her career life, she was a dedicated stay-at-home mom to her two beautiful and accomplished children.

Christi became a nurse once her children went to college and continues nursing today. With her strong faith in Christ and passion for helping others, she now loves serving as a nurse on mission trips. She is an avid artist and paints with watercolor and acrylic. Health and fitness are also an important focus for her and a daily way of life.

About Dr. Joe Pecoraro

Dr. Joe Pecoraro is known throughout the world as "Dr. Joe." He earned a BA in zoology, followed by an MD degree from the University of South Florida, and is board certified by the American Board of Surgery. While practicing general and vascular surgery, his articles appeared in numerous surgical publications.

Dr. Joe is a devoted Christian, husband, and father. Both his interest in science and his desire to help relieve the suffering of people compelled him to become a surgeon. This humanitarian drive expanded to the mission field and led him to become one of the three co-founders of Hearts Afire, Inc. Presently, he serves as a working CEO, President, and Chairman of the Board.

On his first mission trip, Dr. Joe saw the hopelessness in the eyes of the people and realized that, inspired by the compassion of God, he had the opportunity to help restore hope, both spiritually and through physical healing. Tireless, visionary, and casual but focused, Dr. Joe is known everywhere as someone "who gets things done." He has not only been the directing force on the forty mission trips which he has led, but his cultural awareness brings comfort to the leaders in the nations in which Hearts Afire serves.

God has given him a remarkable depth of love and the ability to see the beauty and value in those who are needy and the needs of those who appear beautiful and important. By seeking God's desires in the circumstances of his life and leadership, he has learned to give all that God asks and accept all that He offers.

Currently, Dr. Joe and his wife Rhonda are entrepreneurs, helping
thousands of people to achieve both physical and financial health in
their lives. This mode of business gives him the opportunity, in his
"downtime," for jogging (preferably barefoot on the beach), kayaking,
hiking mountains, reading, and mentoring others, spiritually and in
business. He roasts his own coffee from organic beans that he obtains
from the countries he travels to with Hearts Afire.

Connect with Dr. Joe:

Facebook: www.facebook.com/joe.pecoraro.790
Hearts Afire Facebook: www.facebook.com/heartsafire.us/
Email: jpecoraro@heartsafire.us
Instagram: @drjoepecoraro
Twitter: @joepecoraro
Websites: www.heartsafire.us
             www.yourvibrantlifenow.com

About Rhonda Pecoraro

Rhonda Pecoraro is Co-founder and Chief Operating Officer of Hearts Afire, Inc. and Co-founder of Your Vibrant Life Now, Inc. Rhonda earned her Bachelor of Arts degree in Fine Arts (painting and photography) from the University of South Florida in Tampa. She is an active member of the National Association of Christian Women Entrepreneurs (NACWE).

By combining her dual passions of photography and missions, she effectively captures the bond between Hearts Afire team members and the people they serve around the world. "I don't want to just capture a person at a moment in time when I take a photo. I want to capture their heart and who they are."

Rhonda is motivated not only by the hardships she sees on the mission field, but also by her fellow team members' sacrificial willingness to give of themselves, their time, and their finances. She believes that by serving together as a team, Hearts Afire is changing the world.

Rhonda is an advocate to those less fortunate. She is a cheerleader to those who are hurting. She cherishes her roles of a caring and loving wife, mother, sister, daughter, aunt, and friend. She is an author, visionary, and a focused and disciplined leader. She loves living healthy, walking on the beach, and painting in watercolor.

Rhonda serves in a variety of ways for Hearts Afire, including Annual Benefit Chairperson, mission trip co-leader, trip and team organizer, photo editor and documenter of mission trips, and business planner. As a health entrepreneur in her coaching business, she inspires and helps others achieve their health and business goals. By coming alongside and assisting others to achieve their goals, she empowers them to be the best they can be.

Rhonda's mission is this: To encourage others to take their God-ordained vision of doing missions and put their hearts into action.

Connect with Rhonda:

Facebook: www.facebook.com/rhondaspecoraro
Facebook: facebook.com/heartsafire.us for mission updates, mission photos, inspired living, and to stay connected.
Email: rpecoraro@heartsafire.us
Websites: www.heartsafire.us
          www.yourvibrantlifenow.com

About Dr. Vilma Vega

Dr. Vilma Vega, a board-certified infectious disease physician and HIV specialist, is CEO and President of Vega Consulting LLC. As a consultant, she was the prior Chief Medical Officer for the Community AIDS Network (CAN) and is now the Medical Director for their Clearwater clinic. She is also a consultant for Infectious Disease Associates in Sarasota, Florida and various pharmaceutical companies for whom she serves on their speaker bureaus.

Dr. Vega, a Peruvian-born American, decided at age five to become a doctor when her mother was diagnosed with a brain tumor. By age seven, she desired to become a missionary after watching humanitarian efforts on TV. Over time, she realized the God-ordained purpose for her life— to combine her love of medicine with her passion for missions. This, along with her love for people, led her to co-found Hearts Afire, Inc. in 2006. She is currently an active board member, President Emeritus, and a spokeswoman for Hearts Afire. She continues to serve on the mission field, leading teams and inspiring others to dedicate their lives to Christian service. God has given Dr. Vega the gift to speak biblical truth, burning the message of missions in the hearts of many so they can actively fulfill God's great commission and pursue their divine purpose. Dr. Vega continually aspires to be the hands and feet of Jesus, encouraging and leading through God's Word and Christ's example. Her impact is evident in every individual who crosses her path and is transformed by the power of the Holy Spirit. She passionately seeks God and inspires others to live their spiritual lives to the fullest.

Dr. Vega is a powerful internationally-known motivational speaker on the subjects of health and wellness, global missions, HIV/AIDS, and infectious diseases. She is frequently requested by national, regional, and faith-based media for expert commentary on medical news in the United States and around the world. She loves to share testimonies of her life and the principles of the Balanced Life Blueprint. One of her personal quotes is, "Shape your life or your life will be shaped for you."

Dr. Vega received her MD from the University of Illinois and completed her infectious disease residency and fellowship at Jackson Memorial Hospital/University of Miami. She holds a Bachelor of Science from Loyola University and a Bachelor of Ministry from Christian Family Church International.

Connect with Dr. Vilma:

Facebook: www.facebook.com/vilma.vega.775
Hearts Afire Facebook: www.facebook.com/heartsafire.us/
Email: vegaconsultinggroup@gmail.com
Websites: www.heartsafire.us
*   www.vilmavega.com*

Join Our Hearts Afire Family!

Have you felt a nudge or seen yourself as being part of something big that benefits others?

Do you want to serve on an international mission trip?

Is experiencing and discovering your faith in new and meaningful ways something you desire?

Wherever God is calling, Hearts Afire has a place for you!

Hearts Afire was born out of a passion to serve those in great need worldwide. Since 2006, Hearts Afire has been sending mission-minded individuals like you from all walks of life into the world in the name of Christ. Teams of people committed to serve together use their gifts, skills, and resources to impact the world through short-term missions and sustainable projects.

Nations where God has called Hearts Afire:

Peru	Dominican Republic
Haiti	Ghana
Kenya	Uganda
Tanzania	Swaziland
India	Philippines
Honduras	

Where do you see yourself?

Children's Programs

- Giving big hugs to the little children
- Serving in an orphanage
- Teaching Bible stories and crafts
- Playing soccer and sharing the salvation story
- Washing children's feet and fitting them with new shoes

Medical Teams

- Working in a rural medical clinic
- Evaluating people for reading glasses
- Working in dental hygiene and dentistry
- Assisting in pharmacy
- Performing lab tests

Ministry Teams

- Praying with a translator
- Distributing Bibles

Other Ways You Can Serve

- Serving meals to children and families
- Building sustainable projects
- Distributing hygiene bags

We see the value of leaving a legacy. The continual blessings that our sustainable projects provide make an ongoing impact in the lives we come in contact with long after our teams return home.

How can you become part of Hearts Afire?

- Pray for the ministry
- Encounter God with us on the mission field
- Experience the blessings of being a donor
- Invest in a sustainable project
  - o Wells, orphanages, churches
  - o Hearts Afire Mountain Medical Center – Eldoret, Kenya

We invite you to visit www.heartsafire.us and join the Hearts Afire family today!

CPSIA information can be obtained
at www.ICGtesting.com
Printed in the USA
FSOW04n0934240217
31175FS